A POSTCARD FROM
THE LICKEYS

For our friend Joan Dunn who shares our enthusiasm for postcards
and the Lickey Hills. Thank you for your encouragement.

A POSTCARD FROM THE LICKEYS

THE LICKEY.

The "Beauties" of The Lickey
cannot be exaggerated.
Too busy to write.

By

JOE & FRANCES BRANNAN

First published in April 1989 by
K. A. F. Brewin Books, Studley, Warwickshire

Reprinted July 1989

ISBN 0 947731 53 9

Typeset in Worcester Round
by Litho Link Ltd, Welshpool, Powys, Wales

**Printed and bound in Great Britain at
The Camelot Press Ltd, Southampton**

Introduction

A POSTCARD FROM THE LICKEYS

For many years The Lickey Hills have been a favourite recreation spot for the people of Birmingham and the surrounding population.

In the 18th century, Lickey Common, an area of around 3000 acres, was a "common" in the true sense covered with forests and heath land. In the early 19th century this common area was gradually reduced until the whole of it was enclosed except for a small part on which the Rose & Crown stands. That area was enclosed in 1883, so unfortunately the whole area became privately owned.

The Birmingham Association for the Preservation of Open Spaces and the Cadbury family began a campaign to aquire this land and give it to Birmingham Corporation for the enjoyment and use of the general public.

Rednal Hill was bought and handed over in 1889. Gradually the greater part of the Hills was purchased or given to the City, until an area of about 450 acres was once more "Common land".

It is our intention to evoke memories of past visits to the Lickeys and ensure future interest with the hope that the area will remain unspoilt by encroaching developments.

Most "Brummies" have a great love of the Lickeys, so we hope that they will enjoy this look through some of our collection of postcards and photographs in . . .

A Postcard from the Lickeys

CHAPTER ONE

Barnt Green

In June 1840 the Birmingham and Gloucester line of the Midland Railway opened from the south to Bromsgrove and on the 17th September 1840, the continuation of this line was opened to Cofton Farm near Barnt Green. This made the village a useful departure point for a tour of the Lickeys. Having crossed the line it was a short walk along the footpath over the fields to Pinfield Woods.

For quite some time this was the only means of public transport from Birmingham to the Hills.

The village itself was much smaller than it is today. When the Railway arrived, Barnt Green gradually grew as a commuter residential area for the City and has continued to do so ever since.

The village of Barnt Green sprang up as a result of the advent of the railway.

S 11681   MIDLAND RAILWAY STATION. BARNT GREEN.

Barnt Green station was built in 1846 by request of the Windsor-Clive family of Hewell Grange, to be used by their tenant farmers.

The modern view has not changed too much.

This postcard was sent in 1915 to a collector of railway station views.

Between Barnt Green and Blackwell stations lies the famous 300 ft. Lickey Incline. To climb this slope trains required the assistance of extra engines known as Bankers.

STATION ROAD, BARNT GREEN

On leaving the station, visitors bound for the Lickey Hills would cross Station Road and take to the fields. This road is now known as Fiery Hill Road.

Station Road, Barnt Green.

It is doubtful whether there was enough crime in Barnt Green to merit as large a Police Station as this. Indeed it no longer has a Police Station, only Police houses on Bittel Road.

The wealthy Birmingham business people who had large houses built in this area, were able to travel by train into the city.

The Station entrance on Hewell Road leads to the village shops and Post Office.

The buildings may not be much changed but the state of the roads and pavements has definitely improved!

"Messenger" Series.

The Lickey.　　　　　Hewell Road, Barnt Green.

Barnt Green   *The Village*

We may complain about the state of the roads nowadays but they are a vast improvement on the turn of the century.

S 11678   HEWELL ROAD, BARNT GREEN.

In 1910 the sender of this card said "We look right across the fields out of the shop windows, lovely country." Nowadays these fields are all built upon.

Barnt Green House was formerly the home of the land agent to the Windsor-Clive family of Hewell Grange. It is now the Barnt Green Inn.

135/2 **The Grange and Gardens, Hewell, Redditch**

This card was sent to Maine, USA in 1939. "Have been to see this garden this afternoon — the flowers almost all blue — great delphiniums. There is a private chapel in the house with lapis lazuli floor — Tapestry in the great hall copied from some in the museum in Paris."

The last Earl of Plymouth to own Hewell Grange died in 1943. It was sold to the Government for use as an approved school and is now one of H.M. Youth Custody Centres to which there is no public access unless one meets the requirements for a "visit"!

125/9 **The Cross Roads, Barnt Green**

Many of these quiet corners have been lost to development. However, not everyone found it a pleasure to stay here. The message reads "Cherry Croft, Barnt Green. Am stuck here 'til the 19th, never came to a more benighted hole in my life! Not a house nor shop nor boy for miles! Lovely woods for spooning but nothing to do it with!!"

Just as the coming of the railway created the original impetus for development in the area, so has the opening of the M42 linking the M5 with Nottingham. Those once quiet lanes are again being rapidly developed.

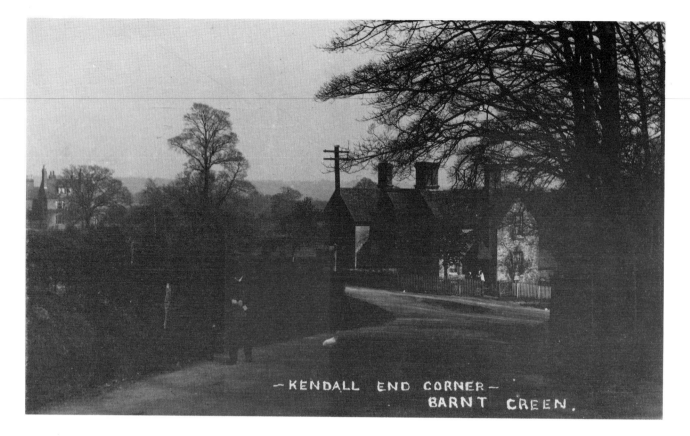

This quiet rural scene bears little resemblance to the busy road of the 1980's. Indeed, both man and hen would soon come to an untimely end if they ventured out onto the road today.

Kendal End, Barnt Green.

The Barnt Green cattle market took place on Wednesdays. It was held in the area now occupied by the old people's bungalows (Longlands) off Hewell Lane. It closed down about 30 years ago. This card, sent in 1910, was loaned by George Sawyer.

Notice how the name Cofton has been mispelt Coston. This may be due to the confusion between s and f on the old maps.

The huge dray horses pause for a rest by the pool near the Tower House.

CHAPTER TWO

Rubery

On September 10th, 1883, the Halesowen Joint Midland and Great Western Railway line was opened. This was another link with the Lickey Hills by public transport. The only other form of transport at this time was the carrier's cart from Bromsgrove to Birmingham.

Rubery Station was at the bottom of Holly Hill about half a mile from the Village. The site of this now holds a shopping area on the Frankley Estate.

The railway afforded visitors an easier access to Rubery Hill Lunatic Asylum, opened in 1850. A road from the station joined Bedlam Lane, now Rubery Lane, to bring visitors to the rear entrance of the hospital grounds. A longer walk down Cock Hill Lane took people to the front gate. Regular exercise from walking was deemed necessary for the physical health of the patients so they were allowed to walk over the hills and lanes.

At the turn of the century Rubery was a very small village at the foot of the Lickey Hills, surrounded by fields and farms. The changes to the whole area were dominated by "The Austin". When Herbert Austin bought the small factory at Longbridge in 1905 he started more than just a car factory. He opened up a whole new way to the Hills with the motor car.

Greetings from Rubery.

"HADDON SERIES"

Passenger trains between Halesowen & Kings Norton stopped at Rubery. There were 5 trains per day. It was necessary to change trains at Kings Norton to get to Birmingham. This passenger service ended in 1919 but the line did not actually close until July 6th 1964. It was used for goods trains and a works service to Longbridge.

Railway sidings laid in 1902 to carry sand and stone from Holly Hill quarry to the construction site of Frankley Reservoir.

At the turn of the century, the main form of local transport was horse drawn. You could hire various forms of horse drawn vehicles to carry you around the Hills. Three of Rubery's public houses had stables, including the New Rose & Crown. There were also two blacksmiths.

The tram service from Birmingham only ran as far as Selly Oak. 1913 saw the beginning of an extension of this service in the form of open topped motor buses, to Rubery & Rednal.

In 1926 the tramway was extended as far as Rubery. The No. 71 tram had its terminus near Rubery Hill Hospital entrance.

The tram track ran along what is now the central reservation of Bristol Road South. The service continued up till 1952 when buses took over.

Rubery Hill Lunatic Asylum opened for patients on January 4th 1882. It was built for the overspill from Winson Green Asylum. It cost £133,495.5s.8d. to build & equip. Mainly permanent or hopeless cases were put in the hospital. Out of 452 patients 78 men & 70 women were epileptics and kept separate from other patients.

On May 6th 1905, Hollymoor Hospital opened as an Annexe to Rubery Hill.

A walk in the Lickey Hills was part of the treatment for some patients. The message on one postcard from the Lickeys in 1906 said "I wish I was having another week here I do have some fun with the lunies give them some bacca there all right".

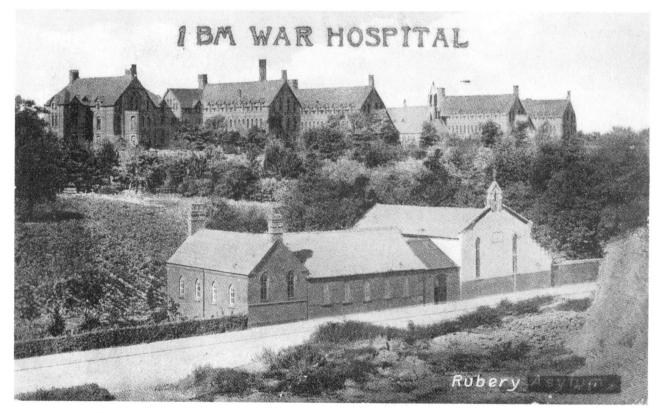

Rubery Hill was occupied by the War Office till 1919. The hospital was adapted and equipped for the sick and wounded soldiers. This cards message of June 29th 1916 reads. "I have been outside this afternoon. Have got the bandages off at last."

1ST BIRMINGHAM WAR HOSPITAL & CAMP, RUBERY.

Much reconstruction work took place after the war. New buildings were added, including a Male Nurses home, which later became the Nurse Training Centre. The War Office paid £25000 and the city authorities spent a further £60000 to bring the hospital up to standard. Very little work had been done during the War as there was a shortage of labour.

BEACON HOSTEL REDNAL

J.H.Austin

This view of the junction of Lickey Road and Bristol Road South is greatly changed by blocks of flats.

Once the transport service with Birmingham was improved in 1926 the area was rapidly developed. Much of the farm land was sold and built upon. It remains a very busy route since it links the M5 and M42 motorways with the city.

In 1905 Herbert Austin bought a derelict factory where he started his motor car manufacturing business. He tested his first car on the Lickeys in 1906. The company struggled to survive at first but by 1910, the Austin company employed over a thousand workers. During the First World War the factory switched to munitions work and the work force rose to 20,000 but the company was almost bankrupt. He saved the situation with a new car — the Austin Seven.

The modern works are still being expanded.

4232   HOMEWARD BOUND FROM THE AUSTIN WORKS   AERO PICTORIAL LTD. 136 REGENT STREET. W. 1

PRE WAR Photo.

The factory has continued to grow. It spread across the Bristol Road and up Lickey Road and Lowhill Lane. The traffic generated by the works at the end of the afternoon is still overwhelming by comparison.

W H DAY, Copyright   THE LICKEY HILLS.   Birmingham
NAZARETH HOUSE, LONGBRIDGE.

Nazareth House was opened in 1912. It was an orphanage of Roman Catholic children but is now used as an old people's home.

RUBERY HILL, RUBERY

In the days before the Rubery by-pass was built, Dales bakery stood on the corner of Leach Green Lane and New Road.

A bridge forded the Callow Brook and Cock Hill Lane took its winding route over the hill to the Cock Inn.

This spot is now unrecognisable. The road is now completely built up with tower blocks of flats, maisonettes and houses.

The Congregationalist Chapel was built in 1841 as a Methodist Chapel. It was near the Rubery end of Cock Hill Lane in front of the Asylum. It was destroyed by fire in 1959.

SPRING POOLS, RUBERY. No. 292

Much of this scene is changed by the By-Pass road leading to the Motorway although some of the pools can still be seen from the road.

The land around Rubery was mainly farm land. This rural scene was photographed by a Rubery photographer.

Rubery village expanded gradually and the roads were improved. It is said that the prisoners of war during the First World War tarmaced the road.

Rubery in the early forties had become a larger "village" with shops and parking spaces more suitable for the housing area it now served.

This card was sent to Scotland in Oct. 1944.
"Spending my leave here weather is OK. Have to report back at camp Thursday and as far as I know I am going to London Friday" ... "no sign of you coming back" ... "I had a letter from J. S. from France and she seems to be enjoying herself I wish it was all over" ...

Between the wars Birmingham improved its housing and built new council estates. The land between the "Austin" and Rubery was gradually filled with houses.

R 8   NEW ROAD. RUBERY   A WYNN CARD

This card sent in 1960 does not really reflect how much change had taken place around Rubery. In the fifties the trams had disappeared and tower blocks of flats and council estates had further encroached on the green belt. The village had become a more important commercial area.

The Plough was one of four public houses in Rubery at the turn of the century. At that time it had stables. Perhaps the number of visitors passing through Rubery to and from the Lickeys reflected the need for so many pubs.

The Plough is now separated from the rest of the village by the fly-over.

The original wooden Church of St. Chads was dedicated in 1895. It has been replaced by a modern brick building on the same site. This view was sent in July 1917 to Selly Oak and the message says "Glorious weather out here haymaking is a treat."

S. Chad's Church, Rubery.

Rubery has had a Social Club for a long time. Attitudes have obviously changed over the years as it must be noted that there are no women present even though it is a festive time.

From Rubery village it is an uphill walk to the Lickey Hills. The lower hillside has gradually become built up. This scene is now much changed by the Valley Farm Estate.

The Agatha Stacey Homes are in Eachway Lane. There was a large Laundry there at some time but now it is a home for handicapped people.

A cross on this card notes that the building in the distance with a white fence is the home or workplace of the sender. The message reads "Home for inebriates (Laundry! Work) B'ham City". One can but imagine the meaning of such a remark.

Eachway or Etchey was a hamlet marked on deeds and plans as long ago as the 16th century. The group of houses eventually became part of Rubery.

Beacon Hill Lane is a continuation of Eachway and winds its way onto the Lickey Hills.

I'M ALWAYS THE GENTLEMAN
At Rubery

CHAPTER THREE

Rednal & Cofton

For the purposes of this book we define the place we call Rednal as the village at the foot of Rednal Hill, the area now the site of Rose Hill roundabout and Leach Green Lane. Cofton comprises the common, the cottages at the top of Groveley Lane, the Lane itself, Ten Ashes and the land and houses across from Cofton Church.

In 1913, Rednal saw the advent of the open topped bus which linked Birmingham and the Lickeys. This was the fore-runner to the tram which arrived here in 1924. Now it was possible to travel all the way from Navigation Street to Rednal. The journey was so popular that the terminus needed enlarging. The following year a large loop was constructed and the terminus made more attractive by gardens and an ornate shelter. This became a famous landmark for Brummies arriving for a day at the Lickeys. Sadly it is no longer there.

The Twilight Hour in
Lickey Hills, Rednal

THE LICKEY HILLS, REDNAL. NEAR BIRMINGHAM.

COPYRIGHT

532 A

In 1911, Rednal became part of Birmingham. The open-topped motor bus continued the City tram service out to Rednal in 1913 thus making the Lickey Hills even more accessible to the public.

MOTOR TERMINUS REDNAL

JOHNSON & GIBBS. RUBERY.

At the turn of the century there were four public houses in Rednal all of which were situated in the same locality as the bus terminus. Perhaps one needed sustenance after a journey on an open-topped bus!

The Barracks Inn stood on the site now occupied by Clark's Motor Services. It was demolished in the 1920's.

A scene once dominated by public houses is now much changed by the busy traffic from Clark's Motor Services.

The Hare and Hounds, Rednal.

Only one of the original public houses can still be visited – The Hare & Hounds. It was, and still, a popular place. The frontage has changed very little.

Rednal Tram Terminus.

The tramway was extended from Selly Oak to Leach Green in 1924. It was such a popular route that the terminus had to be enlarged. In 1925, a 200 yard loop was constructed outside the City boundary. A wrought iron and glass shelter was built too.

The popularity of the Lickeys is obvious judging by this queue for the tram on Easter Monday 1931.

With the onset of the Second World War, tram rides to the Lickeys must have been even more valued as an outing, due to war time limitations on travel.

In the middle distance stands a camouflaged war-time tram car. This view was photographed in May 1943.

Trams continued to run to the Hills until the early 1950's. Many Birmingham people remember the bone-shaking journey with great affection.

LS 7   REDNAL VILLAGE, LICKEY HILLS, BIRMINGHAM

1952 saw the last tram car to the Lickeys. The buses took over. With the increase in motor car ownership and the ability to travel further afield, other attractions were sought to bring in the visitors.

FOUR WAYS REDNAL

It is hard to imagine that the top of Groveley Lane with the modernised Chalet Public House, could ever looked like this.

THE FOUR WAYS, REDNAL.

It was the increased use of the motor car which brought about the drastic changes here. The fashions at the turn of the century were hardly conducive to hill walking!

Our favourite postcard! How did they ride on the Hills like that?

The Barnt Green Road is on the left. This view no longer exists. The cottages are gone and the road much changed by the roundabout at the bottom of Rose Hill.

Post Office, Rednal, The Lickeys.

Some of the little group of shops in Rednal village still exist but there is no longer a Post Office.

ROSE COTTAGE, REDNAL.

This cottage was on Lickey Road between the Post Office and the Hare & Hounds. An advertisement in "Bradmore's Guide to the Lickey Hills" says "Cyclists and parties should stop at Harris's Tea Rooms, Rose Cottage Rednal. Headquarters of the Carlton Cycling Club. Parties, choirs and classes accommodated with tea at shortest notice."

This scene of bustling activity in Rednal Village shows just how popular it was for a day trip.

To stand in the middle of Lickey Road posing for a photograph was much less hazardous in 1913. Indeed he would probably be flattened by a car transporter today.

The sender of this card addresses it from The Ten Ashes Cottage, Rednal, Barnt Green. 20th Sept. 1910 5.30 pm. "Cycled here on Albert's m/c & have just had T & are just off back again."

The little group of original cottages still retain their charm. (and value!)

The Johnson family lived at Cofton Cottage. Local people still remember buying sweets at the cottage window.

How much of our postcard collection was originally bought here? What an array of souvenirs!

A large number of these pretty cottages have long since been demolished. The owners provided jugs of tea for many thirsty visitors.

By all accounts Rose Cottage was an extremely popular name for houses in this region and most houses served refreshments to visitors.

Life at Ivy Cottage is an integral part of the novel "Merry Hearts at Rednal" by Marianne Hipkins published in 1935. Her romantic story set in the Lickey Hills tells of the way people may have lived in this area. The book can be found in the Local Studies Section of Birmingham's Central Library.

REDNAL, FROM HIGH PARK

High Park, now known as Cofton Park, was farmland until it was made public in 1936.

HIGH PARK, REDNAL.

Lowhill Farm worked the land on Cofton Park. Some of the field boundries can still be seen. The old farmhouse still stands in the middle of the park. 1910 2nd Aug. "Having a fine time here. We all went hay making yesterday. It is very windy here today. I hope it goes down. We are going to a flower show at Rednal tonight."

H. 207.   ON THE LICKEYS. BIRMINGHAM.

This view from the slopes of Cofton Park is still recognisable but the building of the Chalet changed the middle of the scene.

REDNAL, FROM TEN ASHES

Recent years saw the development of this area as a housing estate. It is now impossible to find this view.

"SCOTT" SERIES, No. 642

LOVERS LANE THE LICKEY HILLS N° BIRMINGHAM.

How many treasured memories are evoked by this view?

Cofton & Lower Bittell reservoirs were constructed in 1790's by the Birmingham & Worcester Canal Company to guarantee water for mills. The River Arrow was dammed in two places. Eventually the canal needed water to keep its summit level full so another reservoir was constructed.

Cofton Reservoir is the only one of the three reservoirs wholly in the Parish of Cofton. Water from here and the Lower Bittell Reservoir had to be steam pumped to the level of the Upper Bittell Reservoir before it could be used to feed the canal.

COPYRIGHT L L H   COFTON CHURCH.   152 A

Cofton Church stands near to Cofton Hall. It was probably built as a chapel for Robert de Leycester (Lord of the Manor) in 1330. Some of the original walling still remains.

COFTON HACKET CHURCH

In 1880 St. Michael's Church, Cofton Hackett, became a Parish Church. Previously the community was too small to merit its own vicar and services were taken by a priest from Northfield.

The Retreat, Lickey Hills, (Newman's Resting Place.

In 1851 John Henry Newman brought his community of priests to Hagley Road, Edgbaston. He was 50 years old. Soon after, he began to look for a place for a cemetery for his community — the Congregation of the Oratory. He found a place on the Lickey Hills.

CARDINAL NEWMAN'S GRAVE, REDNAL, Nr. BIRMINGHAM.

The land was at the corner of Leach Green Lane and Lickey Road. They had a cottage built in 1854 and the first burial took place there in 1855.

The Crucifix, Cardinal Newman's Chapel, Rednal

Newman was so happy with his Retreat House he used to walk the 8 miles from Edgbaston to visit it.

Grave of Cardinal Newman, The Retreat, Rednal

He was made a Cardinal in 1879.
After a long, fullfilling life he died in 1890 and was buried in the grounds of the Retreat House.

This view of Leach Green Lane was sent in 1907. The sender explains that they live in the cottage in the dip behind John Till the postman. The postman is standing by his own house.

This postcard was posted at 10.30 am to Sparkhill with the message asking someone to be at Station Street by 8.30 pm. The postal service was so much more efficient in those days!

This view of the junction with Lickey Road is now changed by houses and Rednal Postal Sorting Office.

The message on this card reads "Beacon Cottage, August 1910. We leave here tomorrow morning. I shall have to wish this sweet spot a long lingering farewell. Went to Birmingham yesterday. So hot. In Pattison's, where I had tea, they gave the ladies such pretty little fans for a souvenir."

LEECH GREEN LANE, THE LICKEY HILLS, REDNAL.

Note this mis-spelt name again. Perhaps it has some bearing on the origins of the road name?

There was a field at the corner of Leach Green Lane where a fair was held once a year. Many people can still remember this exciting event.

CHAPTER FOUR

The Lickey Hills

The Lickeys consist of a valley dividing two ranges of hills. On one side is Bilberry Hill, Lickey Warren, Cofton Hill and Pinfield Wood. The higher side comprises Beacon Hill and Rednal Hill. The River Arrow has its source on these hills.

Since 1889, the Lickeys have been increasingly popular as a short holiday resort for the people of the Midlands. With transport developments of this century, it is no longer necessary to consider the nine miles from Birmingham as a great distance to travel. So nowadays, visitors to the hills come mostly for walks and picnics.

Postcard messages show that in the early part of this century people would frequently stay at one of the local houses for a holiday at any time of the year. Most of the houses around the Lickeys took in guests or provided refreshments for visitors.

Our Hill-Climbing Trial at the Lickey Hills

Bilberry Hill Tea-Rooms, The Lickies, near Barnt Green   Valentines Series   50706

At the foot of Rose Hill stands the Bilberry Tea Rooms. Postmarked Selly Oak 14th July 1905. "This is where we went yesterday, we walked there and back. These are the tea rooms which Mr Cadbury gave."

TEA ROOMS & BILBERRY HILL, LICKEY   Nº 35.

Mr & Mrs Barrow Cadbury made the generous gift of these tea rooms in 1904. The building now houses the Bilberry Hill Training Centre. In 1960 the Birmingham Federation of Boy's Clubs took it over and extended it.

This reply was sent in 1913 to an address in Handsworth, Birmingham from the Bilberry Hill Tea Rooms. "We don't let bedrooms this is only a tea place and I don't know of anyone as everyone is nearly always full up for the holidays but you might try Mrs Daniels, Hill Cottage, Rose Hill, Rednal."

This card was sent to Ohio, USA in Sept. 1929. "Glad to get your good news. Mother will remember this place. Out for the day with the Sunday school children. Just had a bad thunder storm. Lightning struck a bush and set it on fire."

This gives a inkling of the popularity of the Hills. It is hard to imagine such crowds nowadays. The view of the quarry leaves much to be desired. It is said that 20,000 visitors to the Hills were counted on a Bank Holiday in 1919.

August 20th 1912. "This is one of the hills I have been on. It is lovely here as you can see by the postcard." The sender appears to have fairly low expectations of her holiday views.

The quarry can just be seen in the distance. It was probably stone from these quarries which was used for local road building.

This area was considered the gateway to the Hills.

Old Rose and Crown, Tea Rooms, Rednal

Originally on this site there was a coaching inn where the stage coaches could change horses for the challenging hill climb. When the coaches were re-routed through Rubery the business declined. In 1880 the building was bought by Mr Whenham, a Birmingham accountant, and demolished. He put up the present building and was responsible for landscaping the gardens.

THE OLD ROSE & CROWN INN. LICKEY HILLS.   25218.

The Rose & Crown was made famous in 1869 by Elihu Burritt in "Walks in the Black Country". He arrived from America in June 1846 to make a foot tour of the Black Country. On the first night of his walk he arrived at the Rose & Crown.

S.17916.   THE PARK, LICKEY HILLS.

"I had made a sauntering walk to this little cosy old inn ... It was just the English wayside inn I had read and dreamed of from youth ... Everything in it was thoroughly English, to the watering-trough, the settle under the shade trees, the skittle-grounds, beer mugs and all. And there was the landlady ... a regular Saxon-faced and Saxon-haired woman, buxom, bland and radiant."

LICKEY HILLS.

THE LICKEY HILLS.

DAY. Copyright   The Bridge, Old Rose & Crown Hotel, REDNAL,   Birmingham

The gardens and pools invited visitors from near and far. "August 1925. Motor ride from Brownhills."

THE UPPER FALLS,
THE LICKEY HILLS BIRMINGHAM

The River Arrow was channelled into a series of waterfalls and pools in the grounds of the old Rose & Crown about a hundred years ago. Some of their former glory has been retained.

Golf Links.

The 18 hole Municipal Golf Course was opened in the early 1920's. The Cadbury family were responsible for laying out the course and persuading the City of Birmingham to run it. It was possibly the first such golf course in the country.

THE LICKEY HILLS, REDNAL, SHOWING the MUNICIPAL GOLF LINKS in VALLEY~BIRMINGHAM.

Rose Hill was part of the old stage coach route from Birmingham to Bristol. It was probably part of the Old Roman Saltway from Droitwich.

In 1820 the road was re-aligned but stage coaches still had problems with the steep hill. Eventually a new road was constructed in 1831 which took an easier route from Longbridge via Rubery. The road is still called "New Road".

The River Arrow has its source in the Hills. It flows under this bridge and through Cofton to join the river Avon.

THE STEPS, REDNAL HILL.

July 11th 1929
"Having a lovely time here at the Lickey Hills its a beautiful place but its like mountain climbing to go up hills there are seats every few yards up. I'm sunburnt off the hills its great as good as the sea."

THE LICKEY HILLS, GENERAL VIEW.   558 A

1914 "Have been here for the day and had a very nice day. Walked across the fields from Northfield."

THE LICKEY
FROM ROSE HILL

The sender wished her friend Maud could have come on holiday here with her — "I have had a lovely time on the Lickeys each day. Plenty of luck with soldiers."

17th September 1908.
"We are going up this way to tea next Saturday, they are going to fetch us in their trap, when are you coming up?"

April 14th 1911
"We had a lovely ride here this morning. It looked rather dark but we did not get any rain. The house where I am staying is the first one. There are such a lot of people here for the day."

Sunday July 10th 1927
"Went to the top of the Lickey Hills, climbed to the top and sat on a seat. Was just admiring scenery, saw storm cloud gathering, rushed to the foot and darted into the cafe. Roadway flooded."

What wonderful costumes! It must have been very hot after climbing so far dressed in those hats and long skirts. No wonder there were so many tea rooms.

LICKEY HILLS. THE NEW ESTATE. BIRMINGHAM.

The new estate may have been Rubery as this was sent in 1929.

The present day view shows how much more building has taken place since then.

RUBERY POST OFFICE SERIES.

2. "THE PINES" REDNAL HILL

21st August 1902

"It was beautifully sunny in the evening we were on the hills on this card. They are purple with heather. It is delightful country. More like the views you see of Switzerland."

S 11683   ON THE LICKEYS.

9th April 1908
"Have managed to get this far with the assistance of the train."

The photographer has captured the peace and solitude still to be found in these woods and hills.

"Messenger" Series. 775.

THE LICKEY HILLS, REDNAL.

Drinking Fountain erected by the Earl of Plymouth and Subscribers to the North Bromsgrove Fund raised to Celebrate the Coronation of King Edward VII., 1902.

The drinking fountain can be seen across the road from Lickey Church. The card was posted in Bromsgrove on 8th August 1916.

"I hope you are having a good time this lovely weather. I still get good news from France. This, I must say, is not a typical view of the Hills. It's only of interest to horses, and of course, is visited well by children."

Series 1054　　　The Lickey Hills,- The Grounds & Monument (90 feet high.)　　　Thos. Lewis, Photo. Birmingham.

This monument to the sixth Earl of Plymouth was set up in 1834. The inscription on the plinth reads:—
ERECTED BY THE WORCESTERSHIRE REGIMENT OF YEOMANRY CAVALRY TO MARK THEIR LASTING GRATITUDE TO THE HONOURED MEMORY OF THEIR BELOVED AND LAMENTED COLONEL COMMANDANT AND BY THE COUNTY AT LARGE TO COMMEMORATE THE DISINTERESTED SOLID AND EFFICIENT PUBLIC SERVICES AND COMMEND TO IMITATION THE EXEMPLARY PRIVATE VIRTUES OF OTHER ARCHER SIXTH EARL OF PLYMOUTH.

THE INDICATOR
BEACON HILL, RECREATION GROUND

JOHNSON & GIBBS, RUBERY.

At the summit of Beacon Hill there is a view over several counties. The Indicator is, at present, being reconstructed. Beacon Hill was so called because a network of warning beacons was set up across the country. These were lit to warn of possible foreign invasion.

Although some of this area is now built on there is still a wonderful view of the reservoirs.

ON BILBERRY HILL, Rednal

I wonder if she found many bilberries as she prodded the bushes with her stick?

The Lickey Hills, near Birmingham. Bilberry Hill.   "Scott" Series No.309

With such vast open spaces on the Hills, one can still find a quiet spot to sit and enjoy the fresh air.

This card bears the wonderful message "Sweet memories"! What did it mean? Alas we shall never know!

The photographer inadvertently managed to cast his own shadow on the pathway creating a slightly sinister picture.

Warren Lane has not changed much. It is still a rough road leading to the car park. It has not yet been built up.

Another Rose Cottage!

York Jones tea room was a famous landmark to be reached after a walk over Cofton Hill. Unfortunately there is nothing quite so grand to welcome visitors nowadays.

(On loan from Joan Dunn)

Many can still recall the little fair at Lickey Warren which could be visited all the year round.
1908
"The youngsters are going to have a feast of iced-chips (cocoa-nut). I have had the sport in the shies, so the pleasure will be equal."

THE LICKEY CHURCH.

Holy Trinity Church, Lickey, was erected in 1856.

PARISH CHURCH THE LICKEY

This Gothic style church is on the top of Rose Hill.

"Messenger" Co. Series.

Interior Holy Trinity Church, The Lickey.

When Herbert Austin died in 1941, he was buried in Lickey churchyard. By this time his title was First Baron of Longbridge.

B 11879   LICKEY CHURCH & SCHOOLS

The old school building is still in use as the church hall.

The Lickey Scout Troop was a thriving group right from the start. This photograph may have been taken in the grounds of Herbert Austin's home.

Mr Howitt was the Scout Master and secretary to Herbert Austin. His home was one of the wooden fronted houses opposite the Rose & Crown on Rose Hill. Herbert Austin had these houses built for his staff.

Lickey Scouts "B" Team. 1920-21

The Scout Troop continued to thrive and there is still a group which meets in the Scout Headquarters opposite Lickey Church.

Further reading:

The Story of Rednal. Birmingham Public Libraries.	R. E. Tupling
Rubery — A Guide.	Rubery Historical Society.
Rubery Hill Hospital — A short history.	Peter Tonks & Len Smout
The Windsors of Hewell. Lickey Hills Local History Society.	Margaret Mabey
A Short History of Cofton Hackett. Lickey Hills Local History Society.	Gilbert Herbert & Charles Blount
Merry Hearts at Rednal. Arthur Stockwell Ltd.	Marianne Hipkins
Guide to the Lickey Hills.	Bradmore
Walks in the Black Country 1869	Elihu Burritt